INSIDE THE NHL

San Jose Sharks

Michaela James

AV² provides enriched content that supplements and complements this book. Weigl's AV² books strive to create inspired learning and engage young minds in a total learning experience.

Your AV² Media Enhanced books come alive with...

Audio
Listen to sections of the book read aloud.

Key Words
Study vocabulary, and complete a matching word activity.

Video
Watch informative video clips.

Quizzes
Test your knowledge.

Go to **www.av2books.com**, and enter this book's unique code.

BOOK CODE

H359423

Embedded Weblinks
Gain additional information for research.

Slide Show
View images and captions, and prepare a presentation.

AV² by Weigl brings you media enhanced books that support active learning.

Try This!
Complete activities and hands-on experiments.

... and much, much more!

Published by AV² by Weigl
350 5th Avenue, 59th Floor
New York, NY 10118
Websites: www.av2books.com   www.weigl.com

Library of Congress Control Number: 2014951928

ISBN 978-1-4896-3179-4 (hardcover)
ISBN 978-1-4896-3180-0 (single-user eBook)
ISBN 978-1-4896-3181-7 (multi-user eBook)

Printed in the United States of America in Brainerd, Minnesota
1 2 3 4 5 6 7 8 9 0   19 18 17 16 15

032015
WEP311214

Senior Editor Heather Kissock
Art Director Terry Paulhus

Photo Credits
Every reasonable effort has been made to trace ownership and to obtain permission to reprint copyright material. The publishers would be pleased to have any errors or omissions brought to their attention so that they may be corrected in subsequent printings.

Weigl acknowledges Getty Images and iStock as its primary image suppliers for this title.

San Jose Sharks

CONTENTS

Introduction

San Jose Sharks fans can spend sunny days surfing in the Pacific Ocean and then, at night, enjoy the ice-cold drama of the National Hockey League (NHL). Although it seems an unusual match, hockey is not new to California. In fact, the San Francisco Bay Area was first home to the California Golden Seals, one of six **expansion** teams added to the NHL in 1967. When the Seals left town in 1976, hockey fans in the Bay Area would have to wait 15 long years before the Sharks arrived.

Joe Thornton is an offensive force who is consistently on the ice. In his eight full seasons in San Jose, Thornton has played in all 82 regular season games five times.

Since their very first season in 1991, the Sharks have proven themselves to be a fiery and competitive group, reaching the **playoffs** 17 times in just 23 seasons. The Sharks played in the conference finals in both 2010 and 2011, and entered the 2014 season riding a ten-year streak of playoff appearances. Their hopes are high as they continue their quest for the Stanley Cup.

Patrick Marleau is the Sharks all-time leader in goals, points scored, and games played.

San Jose SHARKS

Arena SAP Center at San Jose

Division Pacific

Head Coach Todd McLellan

Location San Jose, California

NHL Stanley Cup Titles 0

Nicknames Fins, Fish, The Teal Team, Team Teal, Tuna, The Men of Teal

26
All-Star Game nominations

3
Hall of Famers

1
Calder Memorial Trophy

6
Division Championships

History

> **11** The Sharks have had 11 different team captains.

Owen Nolan is one of only six NHL players born in Ireland. He was a key player for the Sharks during his eight years with the team.

From 1967 to 1976, the Oakland Coliseum Arena was home to the California Golden Seals, giving Bay Area residents 11 years to watch and learn about hockey. Unfortunately, the Seals were losing money. This led to Gordon and George Gund III buying the team with the intention of moving it to Cleveland. The team failed in Cleveland as well, and was then moved to Minnesota, where it played as the North Stars.

After a decade of the team being away from San Jose, the Gund family decided it was time to come home, back to the Bay Area. The NHL, however, was against the move. Luckily, former Hartford Whalers owner Howard Baldwin also was set on bringing a hockey team to northern California, and eventually convinced the league to grant him an expansion **franchise** by the Bay. Hockey was reborn in San Jose, although for their first two years of existence, the Sharks played in the Cow Palace, outside of San Francisco. The Sharks did not have to wait long for a home of their own. Their new San Jose arena was completed in 1993 and is now the site of sellout crowds nightly.

The Cow Palace was almost 50 miles (80.5 kilometers) from the Sharks current home in San Jose.

The Arena

When at home, the Sharks enter the rink through a huge shark's head.

Beginning in the 1980s, the city of San Jose was hungry for a new arena and an NHL team to fill it. A group of motivated citizens who called themselves the Fund Arena Now (FAN) pitched the idea of a new arena to sponsors. They convinced the NHL and other investors that San Jose should have a professional hockey arena to attract a new team. The FAN group got their wish shortly thereafter, and construction was underway. Two years later, the arena was finished and named the San Jose Arena, a name that was later changed to the Compaq Center at San Jose.

Another **sponsorship** change in 2002 led to the arena name being changed to HP Pavilion. Currently, the Sharks' home has been renamed the SAP Center at San Jose. Despite all of the name changes, fans most commonly refer to the arena as "The Shark Tank." In addition to hockey, the arena hosts dozens of other ice-based events throughout the year, such as figure skating championships, family events, and college hockey all-star games.

Shark fans never leave hungry when they eat the San Jose classic, bacon-wrapped hot dog.

Where They Play

British Columbia **7**

Alberta **4**

3

CANADA

Saskatchewan

Manitoba **14**

Ontario

Washington

Oregon

Idaho

Montana

North Dakota

Minnesota **11**

Wisconsin

8

South Dakota

Wyoming

Iowa

Illinois

6 SAP Center, San Jose

Nevada

Utah

Colorado **9**

Nebraska

Kansas

Missouri **13**

California

5

1

Arizona **2**

New Mexico

Oklahoma

Arkansas

UNITED STATES

Pacific Ocean

MEXICO

Texas **10**

Louisiana

Miss

Gulf of Mexico

PACIFIC DIVISION

1 Anaheim Ducks
2 Arizona Coyotes
3 Calgary Flames
4 Edmonton Oilers

5 Los Angeles Kings
★ 6 San Jose Sharks
7 Vancouver Canucks

CENTRAL DIVISION

8 Chicago Blackhawks
9 Colorado Avalanche
10 Dallas Stars
11 Minnesota Wild

12 Nashville Predators
13 St. Louis Blues
14 Winnipeg Jets

Newfoundland

Quebec

Prince Edward Island

New Brunswick

New Hampshire

Vermont

Maine

20

Nova Scotia

19

15 Massachusetts

22

26

Rhode Island

27

17

New York

25

Connecticut

Michigan

16

New Jersey

29

Pennsylvania

Ohio

28

Indiana

24

West Virginia

30

Virginia

Delaware

Maryland

District of Columbia

Kentucky

23

North Carolina

Tennessee

South Carolina

12

Alabama

Georgia

Atlantic Ocean

...sippi

Florida

21

18

SAP center
at san jose

Arena
SAP Center at San Jose

Location
525 West Santa Clara Street
San Jose, CA 95113

Broke Ground
June 28, 1990

Completed
September 7, 1993

Features
- Penthouse Terrace suites, featuring HD TVs and luxury dining for 24
- seating capacity of 17,562

LEGEND
- ☆ SAP Center at San Jose
- ■ Eastern Conference
- ■ Western Conference

NHL EASTERN CONFERENCE ★★★

ATLANTIC DIVISION
15 Boston Bruins
16 Buffalo Sabres
17 Detroit Red Wings
18 Florida Panthers
19 Montreal Canadiens
20 Ottawa Senators
21 Tampa Bay Lightning
22 Toronto Maple Leafs

METROPOLITAN DIVISION
23 Carolina Hurricanes
24 Columbus Blue Jackets
25 New Jersey Devils
26 New York Islanders
27 New York Rangers
28 Philadelphia Flyers
29 Pittsburgh Penguins
30 Washington Capitals

The Uniforms

0 Though three Hall of Famers have played for the Sharks, the franchise has yet to retire any jersey numbers.

Prior to 2007, the Sharks wore their white uniforms at home and teal on the road. Currently, the team wears teal at home and white while on the road.

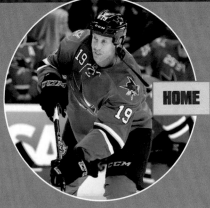

HOME

The Sharks have altered their look only slightly since they joined the NHL. Their uniforms have often been as consistent as their steady on-ice play. From their very first **logo** and uniform design, the Sharks' primary colors were Pacific teal and white. The Sharks wear teal jerseys at home and white jerseys on the road. The primary logo is a shark biting a hockey stick, displaying an intimidating presence.

AWAY

In October 2001, the team's third uniform, or "Black Armor," was introduced. The alternative jerseys are worn at select games, both at home and on the road. In 2007, the NHL revamped many of the league's uniforms, and the Sharks' jersey received a touch-up, with more orange added to its color scheme.

The "Black Armor" jerseys have been worn at home playoff games during recent years. In 2014, though, the team decided to make a change, vowing to use their teal home jerseys for home playoff games going forward.

Helmets and Face Masks

The Sharks have an alternative logo of a shark fin, which is occasionally featured.

TM

Alex Stalock's masks are custom painted, and he often gets new masks for big regular season games or the playoffs.

Of all the rules and traditions that have changed during the NHL's existence, the goaltender's mask may have changed the most. During the league's early years, goalies did not even wear a mask. When masks did arrive, they were nothing more than a dull piece of fiberglass with holes for the eyes and mouth. When goalies began to get creative with their designs, and the masks themselves began to change, a professional art movement in hockey was born.

Current Sharks goaltender, Antti Niemi, has a Pacific teal helmet with a shark logo painted on the chin of his face mask. The team's backup goalie, Alex Stalock, also displays sharks on his mask. Hungry sharks form a circle on Stalock's headgear. The Sharks wear helmets that are clearly black or white, depending on whether they are playing at home or on the road, with a very small Sharks logo beside each player's number.

Anntti Niemi combines team pride with his own unique flair. His helmet has a Sharks logo on the chin and a sword-wielding beast on the side.

The Coaches

4 Of the seven former Sharks coaches, four departed San Jose with a winning record.

With 62 playoff wins, Todd McLellan has more playoff wins than any other Sharks coach.

The San Jose Sharks, like many expansion teams, did not find a quick path, or the ideal coach to guide them, to immediate success. Instead, the team endured some down seasons before finding three very successful coaches who consistently put the Sharks on the brink of a Stanley Cup.

DARRYL SUTTER Darryl Sutter was the first coach to depart San Jose with a winning record. In his five full seasons in San Jose, he successfully directed the Sharks to the playoffs five times. In the 1999–2000 playoffs, his team pulled off a shocking first-round upset, as the eighth-**seeded** Sharks defeated the top-seeded St. Louis Blues.

RON WILSON Ron Wilson replaced Darryl Sutter during the 2002–2003 season, and although the Sharks missed the playoffs that year, Wilson's San Jose team would never miss the playoffs again. In fact, during the next four years in San Jose, Wilson guided the team to at least 43 wins in each and every season. The high point of his stay in San Jose was when the Sharks fell only two wins short of reaching the 2003–2004 Stanley Cup Final.

TODD MCLELLAN Todd McLellan is the third straight successful head coach for San Jose. After joining the Sharks in 2008, McLellan led the team to more victories in his first four seasons than any other coach in NHL history. Under McLellan's leadership, the Sharks have won three Pacific Division titles and also reached the Western Conference final two years in a row. McLellan has the most wins in franchise history and further stretches his lead in that category with each additional victory.

Fans and the Internet

Holding cutouts of shark teeth is just one of the ways the fans have creatively used the shark theme in cheering on their hockey team.

Although Sharks fans put their shark masks away in the off-season, loyal San Jose followers do not stop thinking about the sport, or their Sharks, when hockey season ends. Fear the Fin, at www.fearthefin.com, is an online community for Sharks fans to keep in touch with other like-minded devotees, and occasionally get into a heated debate about their favorite subject, the San Jose Sharks. It is also a place where the most loyal of Sharks supporters can keep a close eye on the standings, player news, and team transactions.

Another popular online place for fans to visit is Blades of Teal, at www.bladesofteal.com. Articles about the team appear daily on this blog and keep fans up to date, almost instantly, on their team. Fans also visit Facebook, Twitter, and Instagram to monitor their favorite players.

Signs
of a fan

#1 Sharks fans love the Jaws theme song, and as it plays throughout the arena, fans open and close their arms to mimic a biting shark.

#2 Shark fans often hold and wave caution flags that warn "Shark Territory."

Legends of the Past

Many great players have suited up for the Sharks. A few of them have become icons of the team and the city it represents.

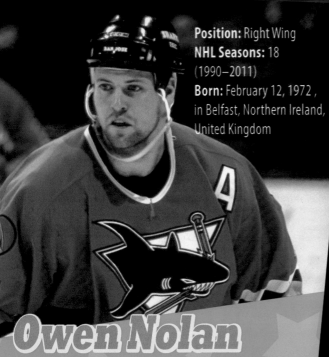

Position: Right Wing
NHL Seasons: 18 (1990–2011)
Born: February 12, 1972, in Belfast, Northern Ireland, United Kingdom

Owen Nolan

As a kid, Owen Nolan immigrated to Canada and took to the ice almost instantly. Nolan was a star in his junior league, but had a rough start when he premiered in the NHL with the Quebec Nordiques in 1990. He became comfortable in his second year, scoring 42 goals, and soon caught the Sharks' attention. He was traded to San Jose in the 1995–1996 season and experienced another bumpy start. He soon settled in, however, scoring 44 goals in the 1999–2000 season while also leading the league in **power play** goals that year.

Dan Boyle

By the time Dan Boyle was acquired by the San Jose Sharks, he was an NHL veteran. A Stanley Cup champion in 2004 with the Tampa Bay Lightning, Boyle was a winner, and the youngsters on the Sharks immediately looked to him for guidance. In his first season in San Jose, he tallied 57 points, with 16 goals and 41 **assists**. He was a powerful player on both sides of the ice, and although his influence extended into the locker room in a very positive way, the team elected not to re-sign him after the 2013–2014 season. Boyle signed a two-year deal with the New York Rangers.

Position: Defenseman
NHL Seasons: 16 (1998–Present)
Born: July 12, 1976, in Ottawa, Ontario, Canada

Jonathan Cheechoo

The Sharks first drafted Jonathan Cheechoo in 1998, but sent him back to the **Ontario Hockey League (OHL)** so he could refine his game. A rising star in the OHL, Cheechoo finally secured a spot on Sharks roster during the 2002–2003 season. Cheechoo scored 28 goals in his second NHL season, nine of which were game winners. In the 2005–2006 season, Cheechoo scored a club record 56 goals, and collected 93 points. He was traded to the Ottawa Senators in 2009.

Position: Right Wing
NHL Seasons: 7 (2002–2010)
Born: July 15, 1980, in Moose Factory, Ontario, Canada

Evgeni Nabokov

In his first 10 NHL seasons, which were all in San Jose, Evgeni Nabokov became the Sharks' all-time leader in just about every goaltending category. To this day, his number of wins and **shutouts** remains unchallenged and unbroken in the Sharks' record books. During his years in San Jose, Nabokov was considered one of the league's very best goaltenders by every measure. Unable to lead his team to the Stanley Cup, despite multiple strong regular season finishes, Nabokov was released by the Sharks in 2010. After three seasons with the New York Islanders, and a short stint with the Tampa Bay Lightning, Nabokov announced his retirement in 2015.

Position: Goaltender
NHL Seasons: 14 (1999–2015)
Born: July 25, 1975, in Kamenogorsk, Kazakhstan

Stars of Today

Today's Sharks team is made up of many young, talented players who have proven that they are among the best in the league.

Patrick Marleau

Patrick Marleau's junior hockey career was brief and promising. After he dominated the Western Hockey League, the Sharks drafted Marleau second overall in the 1997 NHL **Entry Draft**. Considered by some to be the best draft pick in Sharks' history, Marleau has played every game of his NHL career in a Sharks jersey. He currently holds numerous team records, including games played, goals scored, and total points. Although his medal count for Team Canada is lengthy and distinguished, Marleau remains hopeful that the only professional team he has ever known will soon take the final steps to become Stanley Cup champions.

Position: Center/Left Wing
NHL Seasons: 17 (1997–Present)
Born: September 15, 1979, in Aneroid, Saskatchewan, Canada

Joe Thornton

Joe Thornton was an all-star junior player in the OHL and was selected first overall in the 1997 NHL Entry Draft by the Boston Bruins. He slowly grew into a key player in the Bruins' line-up and earned his first 100-point season in 2002–2003. He was traded to the Sharks in 2005, where he and Cheechoo challenged each other to be better players. In the 2006–2007 season, Thornton led the league with 92 assists and 114 points, earning the **Art Ross Trophy** in the process. Thornton is currently the Sharks' all-time leader in assists, and each game provides another opportunity for him to pad his lead in that category.

Position: Center
NHL Seasons: 17 (1997–Present)
Born: July 2, 1979, in London, Ontario, Canada

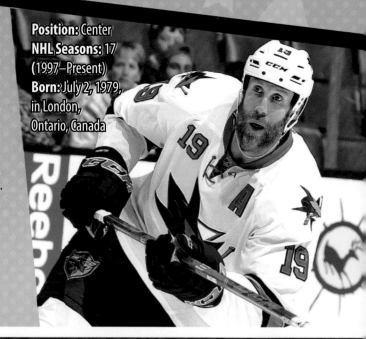

Joe Pavelski

Joe Pavelski was a consistent winner even before joining the Sharks. He was a high school state champion, a champion in the United States Hockey League, and a Division I champion in college. In the 2006–2007 season, Pavelski brought his winning ways to San Jose, and the team has been a steady force in the Pacific Division since he arrived. A silver medalist in the 2010 Olympic Games and only games away from reaching the Stanley Cup Final in San Jose, the American-born center is aiming to take the final steps to make himself a winner on every level of hockey.

Position: Center
NHL Seasons: 9 (2006–Present)
Born: July 11, 1984, in Plover, Wisconsin, United States

Logan Couture

Logan Couture has only played for one professional hockey team during his career, the San Jose Sharks. In the 2009–2010 season, he got his first taste of the NHL, scoring in his first game. In Couture's first full season, he netted 32 goals and collected 56 points. He was second among all NHL **rookies** that year in both goals and points. Since that time, Couture has been an integral part of the Sharks' offensive attack, and the five-year contract extension that he signed with the team in 2013 further ensures that Couture will not be going anywhere else anytime soon.

Position: Center
NHL Seasons: 6 (2009–Present)
Born: March 28, 1989, in Guelph, Ontario, Canada

All-Time Records

443
Most Goals
Patrick Marleau currently holds the team record for goals scored. At the end of the 2013–2014 season, he had scored 443 goals.

92
Most Assists
In the 2006–2007 season, Joe Thornton collected 92 assists, a team record.

954
Most Points
Patrick Marleau holds the team record for points, with 954 at the end of the 2013–2014 season.

53

Most Team Wins

In 2008–2009, the Sharks set the franchise record for most wins, 53, and most points, 117, in a single season.

293

Most Wins as Goaltender

Evgeni Nabokov's number of wins as a Sharks goaltender remains unsurpassed.

Timeline

Throughout the team's history, the San Jose Sharks have had many memorable events that have become defining moments for the team and its fans.

1992
S. J. Sharkie, the club's **mascot**, bursts out and onto the ice for the first time. S. J. works to entertain the Sharks' fan base during this short span of sub par hockey in San Jose.

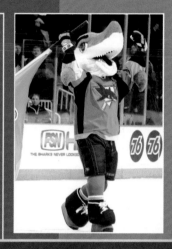

1991
The Sharks play their first game on October 4, 1991. They lose to the Vancouver Canucks.

| 1988 | 1989 | 1990 | 1991 | 1992 | 1993 |

On May 5, 1990, George and Gordon Gund sell their share of the Minnesota North Stars to Howard Baldwin, and the NHL offers the pair an opportunity to own another franchise in San Jose. They gladly accept.

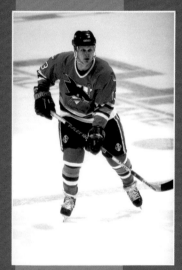

1994
The Sharks, the playoff underdogs, defeat the mighty Detroit Red Wings in a seven-game series. Jamie Baker scores the game, and series, winning goal.

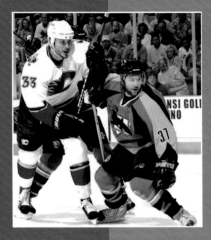

The Future

The Sharks have proven themselves to be consistently competitive. With numerous division titles and almost yearly postseason appearances, San Jose is certainly a worthy NHL franchise. Now, they must take the next steps to join the NHL's elite. Those next steps are a conference championship and a Stanley Cup title.

2004

The Sharks win their second Pacific Division championship. In the postseason, they reach the conference finals for the first time before being defeated by the Calgary Flames.

With a crushing 6–0 defeat of the Stars, the Sharks clinch their 13th playoff berth in 2011.

| 1995 | 2000 | 2005 | 2010 | 2015 | 2020 |

2000

On April 25, the Sharks eliminate the top-seeded Blues in seven games in the first round of the Stanley Cup playoffs. The Dallas Stars end the Sharks' postseason run in the very next series.

2014

After winning the first three games of their first-round series against the Los Angeles Kings, the Sharks let the Kings storm back. Los Angeles, the eventual Stanley Cup champion, wins four straight games to end San Jose's season once again.

Write a Biography

Life Story

A person's life story can be the subject of a book. This kind of book is called a biography. Biographies often describe the lives of people who have achieved great success. These people may be alive today, or they may have lived many years ago. Reading a biography can help you learn more about a great person.

Get the Facts

Use this book, and research in the library and on the internet, to find out more about your favorite Shark. Learn as much about this player as you can. What position does he play? What are his statistics in important categories? Has he set any records? Also, be sure to write down key events in the person's life. What was his childhood like? What has he accomplished off the field? Is there anything else that makes this person special or unusual?

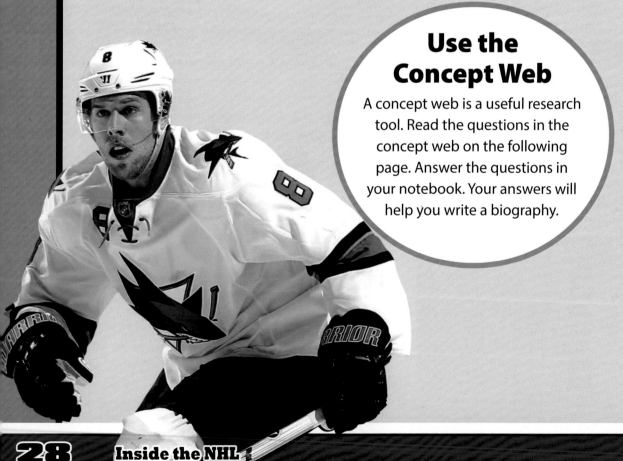

Use the Concept Web

A concept web is a useful research tool. Read the questions in the concept web on the following page. Answer the questions in your notebook. Your answers will help you write a biography.

Concept Web

Adulthood
- Where does this individual currently reside?
- Does he or she have a family?

Your Opinion
- What did you learn from the books you read in your research?
- Would you suggest these books to others?
- Was anything missing from these books?

Childhood
- Where and when was this person born?
- Describe his or her parents, siblings, and friends.
- Did this person grow up in unusual circumstances?

Accomplishments off the Field
- What is this person's life's work?
- Has he or she received awards or recognition for accomplishments?
- How have this person's accomplishments served others?

Write a Biography

Help and Obstacles
- Did this individual have a positive attitude?
- Did he or she receive help from others?
- Did this person have a mentor?
- Did this person face any hardships?
- If so, how were the hardships overcome?

Accomplishments on the Field
- What records does this person hold?
- What key games and plays have defined his career?
- What are his stats in categories important to his position?

Work and Preparation
- What was this person's education?
- What was his or her work experience?
- How does this person work?
- What is the process he or she uses?

Trivia Time

Take this quiz to test your knowledge of the San Jose Sharks. The answers are printed upside down under each question.

1 What is the nickname of the SAP Center?

A. The Shark Tank

2 Who is the current coach of the Sharks?

A. Todd McLellan

3 Which current center won the Art Ross Trophy?

A. Joe Thornton

4 What is the name of the Sharks' mascot?

A. S.J. Sharkie

5 What do the Sharks call their alternative jerseys?

A. Black Armor

6 Which Shark earned the record for most goals in a season? How many goals did he score?

A. Jonathan Cheechoo, 56

7 What is the name of the most prominent blue on the Sharks' jersey?

A. Pacific teal

8 How many division titles have the Sharks won with Todd McLellan as their head coach?

A. Three

9 Which Sharks goaltender has the Shark logo painted on the chin of his face mask?

A. Antti Niemi

Key Words

Art Ross Trophy: a trophy given to an NHL player who has earned the most points by the end of regular season play

assists: a statistic that is attributed to up to two players of the scoring team who shoot, pass, or deflect the puck toward the scoring teammate

entry draft: an annual meeting where different teams in the NHL are allowed to pick new, young players who can join their teams

expansion: expansion in the NHL is marked by the addition of a new franchise. The league last expanded in 2000 when the Columbus Blue Jackets and Minnesota Wild joined the NHL.

franchise: a team that is a member of a professional sports league

logo: a symbol that stands for a team or organization

mascot: a character, usually an animal, that is chosen to represent a team

Ontario Hockey League (OHL): a major Canadian junior hockey league for players aged 15 to 20

playoffs: a series of games that occur after regular season play

power play: when a player from one team is in the penalty box, the other team gains an advantage in the number of players

rookies: players age 26 or younger who have played no more than 25 games in a previous season, nor six or more games in two previous seasons

seeded: a method of ranking teams for postseason play based on regular season records

shutouts: games in which the losing team is blocked from making any goals

sponsorship: to support an NHL team financially in exchange for the promotion of a certain company's products or services

Index

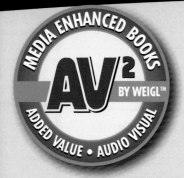

Log on to www.av2books.com

AV² by Weigl brings you media enhanced books that support active learning. Go to www.av2books.com, and enter the special code found on page 2 of this book. You will gain access to enriched and enhanced content that supplements and complements this book. Content includes video, audio, weblinks, quizzes, a slide show, and activities.

AV² Online Navigation

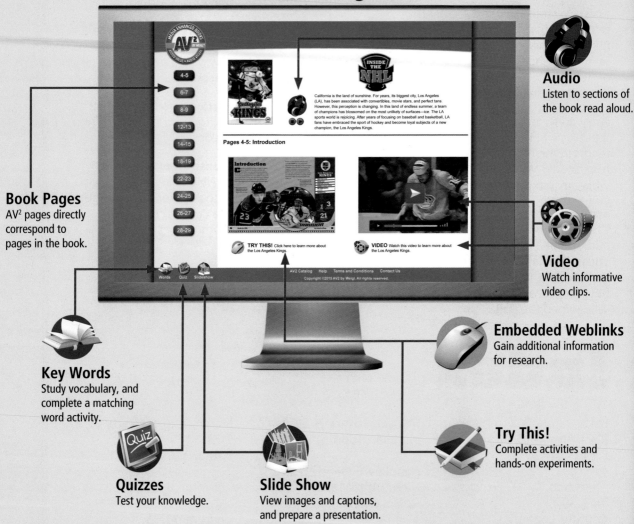

Audio
Listen to sections of the book read aloud.

Book Pages
AV² pages directly correspond to pages in the book.

Video
Watch informative video clips.

Key Words
Study vocabulary, and complete a matching word activity.

Embedded Weblinks
Gain additional information for research.

Try This!
Complete activities and hands-on experiments.

Quizzes
Test your knowledge.

Slide Show
View images and captions, and prepare a presentation.

AV² was built to bridge the gap between print and digital. We encourage you to tell us what you like and what you want to see in the future.

Sign up to be an AV² Ambassador at www.av2books.com/ambassador.

Due to the dynamic nature of the Internet, some of the URLs and activities provided as part of AV² by Weigl may have changed or ceased to exist. AV² by Weigl accepts no responsibility for any such changes. All media enhanced books are regularly monitored to update addresses and sites in a timely manner. Contact AV² by Weigl at 1-866-649-3445 or av2books@weigl.com with any questions, comments, or feedback.